**Senses**

Listening and Hearing

Author's Note

I have worked alongside young children for more than forty years. Over this period I have learned never to be surprised at their perceptive comments about the physical world in which they live. Many of their observations ("Have you seen the crinkles in the elephant's trunk?" "How do seeds know which is their top and which is their bottom?") indicate keen observation and an intuitive use of the senses of taste, touch, sight, smell, and hearing.

The sense-dependent nature of the young child should come as no surprise to parents and teachers. In the early years of life images provided by the senses shape our interpretation of our surroundings and lay the foundations upon which subsequent learning is built. The ideas of hot and cold, far and near, quiet and loud, sweet and sour, soft and hard are developed through the interaction of the child with his or her immediate environment. This interaction encourages observation and questioning which in turn leads to talk and the extension and deepening of language.

This book (like its companions in the series) is a picture book which seeks to encourage both looking and talking. The text may be read by child or adult. Alternatively it may be ignored, the pictures alone being used to trigger an exploration of the child's own insights.

Copyright © 1998, text, Steck Vaughn Company
All rights reserved. No part of this book may be reproduced or utilized in any form or by any means, electronic or mechanical, including photocopying, recording, or by any information storage and retrieval system, without permission in writing from the Publisher. Inquiries should be addressed to:
Copyright Permissions, Steck-Vaughn Company, P.O. Box 26015, Austin, TX 78755

Published by Raintree Steck-Vaughn Publishers, an imprint of Steck-Vaughn Company, a subsidiary of Harcourt Brace & Company

Editors: Helen Lanz, Shirley Shalit
Art Director: Robert Walster
Project Manager: Gino Coverty
Designer: Kirstie Billingham
Photo Researchers: Sarah Snashall

Library of Congress Cataloging-in-Publication Data
Pluckrose, Henry Arthur.
Listening and hearing / by Henry Pluckrose.
    p. cm. -- (Senses)
Summary: Introduces the basic concept of hearing and how it affects our lives.
ISBN: 0-8172-5226-6
1. Hearing--Juvenile literature. [1. Hearing. 2. Senses and sensations.] I. Title. II. Series: Pluckrose, Henry Arthur.
Senses.
QP462.2.P58 1998
612.8'5--dc21
                                97-30963
                                CIP
                                AC
Printed in Malaysia and bound in the United States
1 2 3 4 5 6 7 8 9 0 LB 01 00 99 98 97

Picture credits
Commissioned photography by Steve Shott: cover, title page, 4, 5, 30. Researched photography: Bruce Coleman Ltd 26 (J. Burton); The Image Bank 31 (R. de Aratanha);NHPA 12 (ANT), 13 (S. Krasemann); Unicorn Stock Photos16 (J. Greenberg); Tony Stone Images 19 (A. Sacks), 23 (G. Brad Lewis); Telegraph Colour Library 10-11 (P. Gridley), 22 (G. Shumway), 24-25, 27; John Walmsley 20, 29 (M. Bray); Franklin Watts 8; Zefa 7 (Dann), 9 (Raga), 17 (G.Baden).

Senses

Listening and Hearing

by Henry Pluckrose

RSVP
RAINTREE
STECK-VAUGHN
PUBLISHERS
The Steck-Vaughn Company

Austin, Texas

4

We use our ears to hear
the sounds around us.

We hear faint sounds –
like the sigh of the wind
through long grass
and wheat.

We hear loud sounds –
like the rush
of an express train,
or the sharp ring
of an alarm clock.

We hear low,
continuous sounds –

like the rumble of traffic
along a busy road.

Some sounds
are quite frightening –
like the crack of lightning and
the crash of thunder.

Have you heard a wolf howl?

Some sounds make us smile.

Smiles can lead to laughter.
The sound of people laughing
often makes us laugh too.

We make sounds
for other people to hear.
We talk, sing, and
make music.

Our senses
often work together.
We listen to the band.
We see it, too!

There are some sounds
that we cannot hear at all –
like the sound of a butterfly
drinking from a flower.

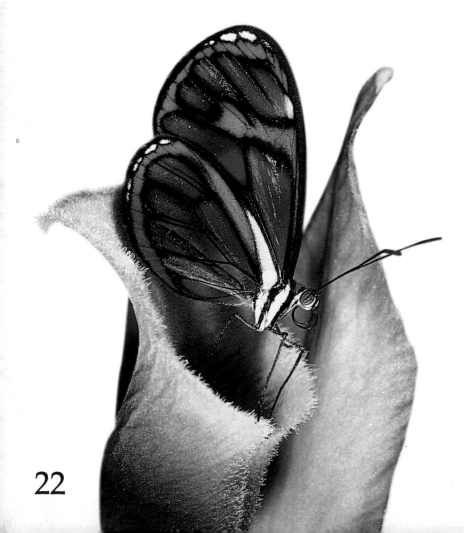

Does snow make a sound
as it falls?

Some materials soften sound. Are your footsteps easy to hear when you run on the beach?

Most living creatures
have a sense of hearing.
Some animals
can move their ears.
This helps them
to hear more clearly.

Can you move your ears?

Sometimes we need
to cover our ears
to quiet loud sounds.
This helps to
protect our hearing.

Without the sense of hearing
our world would be quite silent.
People who cannot hear
sometimes talk with their hands.

Can you hear silence?

Investigations

This book has been prepared to encourage the young user to think about the sense of hearing and the way in which we interpret sounds. Each picture spread creates an opportunity for talk. Sharing talk with a sympathetic adult plays an important part in the development of a child's understanding of the world. Through the subtlety of language, ideas are formed, questioned, and developed.

The theme of hearing might be explored through questions like these:

★ Loud and soft (pp 6-9), Continuous (pp 10-11). What is the faintest natural sound we might hear . . . the sound of raindrops on a flower, the touch of a leaf against the windowpane? What sound can you hear now? Some sounds are continuous, like the sound of a train as it approaches, goes past, and speeds into the distance. What other sounds are continuous in this way?

★ Alarming (pp 12-13). What sounds frighten you most? These may range from a dropped plate to the screaming siren of a police car. Is an unexpected natural sound more frightening than one made by a machine? What kind of sounds are used to give warning or to give a message? (E.g., church bells, clocks striking.)

★ Human sounds and sounds made by instruments (pp 14-21). Human beings communicate through sounds. What sounds make you want to laugh? When a person is crying, what does this tell us about how he or she feels? How many different musical instruments can you name? Do these instruments make high sounds—or very deep ones?

★ Listening (pp 26-27). What shape are human ears? Where are your ears placed on your head? Look at a dog or a cat. Where are its ears placed on its head? What shape are its ears? Look at some pictures of other animals (e.g., elephant, donkey, mouse, deer). How do their ears differ from ours?

★ Protecting the ears (pp 28-29). Why do we sometimes need to protect our ears from sound? Where have you seen ear protectors being used?

★ Sounds of silence (pp 30-31). Encourage a short period of sitting in silence. Can you hear silence?

© Franklin Watts 1997